PAINTINGS OF THE
SOUTHWEST

Edited by Arnold Skolnick • Introduction by Suzan Campbell

Clarkson Potter/ Publishers
New York

A CHAMELEON BOOK

Published by Clarkson N. Potter, Inc.
201 East 50th Street, New York, New York 10022
Member of the Crown Publishing Group.
Random House, Inc. New York, Toronto, London, Sydney, Auckland

CLARKSON N. POTTER, POTTER, and colophon
are trademarks of Clarkson N. Potter, Inc.

Produced by Chameleon Books, Inc.
211 West 20th Street
New York, New York 10011

Production director / designer: Arnold Skolnick
Jacket design: Renato Stansic
Managing editor: Carl Sesar
Editorial assistant: Lynn Schumann
Composition: Larry Lorber, Ultracomp, New York
Printed and Bound by O.G. Printing Productions, Ltd., Hong Kong

CIP information is available upon request from the
Library of Congress.

ISBN: 0-517-59120-0

10 9 8 7 6 5 4 3 2 1

First Edition

(half-title page)
Stuart Davis, *New Mexico Gate*, 1923
Oil on linen, 22 x 32 inches

(frontispiece)
Sheldon Parsons, *October in New Mexico*, n. d.
Oil on canvas, 30 x 40 inches

(title page)
Maynard Dixon, *Cloud World*, 1925
Oil on canvas, 34 x 62 inches

Acknowledgments

From AMERICA by Jean Baudrillard. Copyright © by Jean Baudrillard. Reprinted by permission of Verso / NLB, London and New York.

From PIONEER ARTISTS OF TAOS by Laura M. Bickerstaff. Copyright © 1955, renewed 1983 by Laura M. Bickerstaff. Reprinted by permission of Old West Publishing Co., Denver.

From W. R. LEIGH: THE DEFINITIVE ILLUSTRATED BIOGRAPHY by June DuBois. Copyright © 1977 by June DuBois. Reprinted by permission of The Lowell Press, Kansas City.

From MEMORIES, DREAMS, REFLECTIONS by Carl Jung, edited by Aniela Jaffé. Copyright © 1963 by Random House. Reprinted by permission of Pantheon Books, a division of Random House, New York.

From GEORGIA O'KEEFFE by Georgia O'Keeffe, 1976. Copyright © Juan Hamilton, 1987.

From MASKED GODS: NAVAHO AND PUEBLO CEREMONIALISM by Frank Waters. Copyright © 1950 by Frank Waters. Reprinted by permission of Swallow Press / Ohio University Press.

From MOUNTAIN DIALOGUES by Frank Waters. Copyright © 1981 by Frank Waters. Reprinted by permission of Swallow Press / Ohio University Press.

In the Santa Fe of my childhood, art was everywhere: in our homes; in the studios of artists who welcomed a little girl's endless curiosity and fascination with their magic; in galleries, where children were encouraged to visit and ask questions; and in public spaces. I often visited the Museum of New Mexico's Fine Arts Museum, usually to gaze at Gerald Cassidy's imposing *Cui Bono?* — my favorite painting, then and now. My love for the art of the Southwest is rooted deeply in these early experiences, and I am delighted to have this opportunity to share some of my thoughts on the unique and beautiful contributions to American art made by artists of the Southwest, many of them my lifelong friends.

Creating a book about art is never a solitary pursuit — it is a collaboration among many dedicated people. I want to thank Arnold Skolnick for giving me the opportunity to work with him and his capable staff at Chameleon Books — especially his administrative assistant, Lynn Schumann, and editor, Carl Sesar. Their skill and sensitivity are extraordinary.

To the devoted private collectors and museum curators who generously opened their collections; to the museum registrars, librarians, archivists, and gallery directors throughout the country on whose expertise I relied; and to the art historians whose love of Southwest art is illuminated in their work, I offer heartfelt thanks. I am indebted to the artists who through the years have painted the Southwest, giving us the priceless gifts of their talent and vision.

I am especially grateful to Henry Sauerwein and the Wurlitzer Foundation in Taos, New Mexico, for providing me with the perfect setting for writing about the art of the Southwest. The support of my colleagues at the University of New Mexico and throughout the Southwest, and the loyalty of my friends and family, sustain me. I dedicate this book to my daughter, Rene, whose patient, thoughtful, and loving critiques of my work are invaluable.

Suzan Campbell

This book could not have been possible without the cooperation of the many museums, art galleries and private collectors who supplied the magnificent images in this book.

Of the many public collections we would like to personally thank Joan Tafoya of the Museum of Fine Arts, Museum of New Mexico, Santa Fe, who went beyond the call of duty in getting us images from their Southwest collection; Elizabeth Cunningham, who opened up the files of The Anschutz Collection for us; and Paul Benisek from the Santa Fe Collection of Southwestern Art. We also thank the staffs at the Roswell Museum and Art Center, the Phoenix Museum of Art, the Stark Museum, the Eiteljorg Museum of American Indian and Western Art, the Menil Collection, and the School of American Research.

Gerald Peters from the Gerald Peters Gallery gave us invaluable assistance. We also owe special thanks to Arizona West Galleries; Mitchell, Brown Gallery Inc.; Koplin Gallery; Grace Borgenicht Gallery; Zaplin-Lampert Gallery; The Munson Gallery; Elaine Horwitch Galleries; Frank Croft Fine Art; Hirschl & Adler Modern; Kraushaar Galleries; and Nedra Mattuecci's Fenn Galleries.

We would like to thank all the private collectors, with special thanks to Mr. & Mrs. Bertrand G. Babbitt and The Harmsen Collection.

Thanks to Anne Tamsberg and the staff at Clarkson Potter, and also to Lauren Shakely, who has always believed in me and the series.

It was a joy to work with the author, Suzan Campbell, who wrote the informative text and whose knowledge of the Southwest was incalculable in tracking down the pictures and finding the wonderful quotes in this book.

Special thanks to Lynn Schumann, Nancy Crompton, Jamie Thaman, Joanne Gillett, Halina Rothstein, and Carl Sesar here at Chameleon Books, who put this challenging project together.

And last but not least, thanks to my beloved wife Cynthia who trekked with me through the Southwest researching this book.

Arnold Skolnick

Contents

> "It was always beauty, *always*!...
> The landscape lived, and lived as the world of the gods,
> unsullied and unconcerned. The great circling landscape lived its own life,
> sumptuous and uncaring. Man did not exist for it."
>
> *D. H. Lawrence*, St. Mawr, *1925*

THE SOUTHWEST: MAGIC REGION, PRIMAL SCENE OF THE GREAT AMERICAN MYTH. A MYSTERIOUS, LIVING LANDSCAPE WHOSE MIRAGELIKE BORDERS TANTALIZE, JUST BEYOND GRASP, WHILE ITS VIBRANT EPICENTER—ITS PALPABLE HEART—LIES THROBBING IN THE DESERTS AND MOUNTAINS OF NEW MEXICO AND ARIZONA.

There "...one can hear its slow pulse, feel its vibrant rhythm. The great breathing mountains expand and contract. The vast sage desert undulates with almost imperceptible tides like the oceans," writes Frank Waters, a Southwest visionary.

In this enchanted land—this crucible of dreams, desires, and destinies—artists strive to capture in paint the essence of what D. H. Lawrence brilliantly termed "spirit of place." At first drawn by the infinite aesthetic possibilities of its stunning landscapes and exotic denizens, artists intending only a brief encounter remain, or return again and again, mesmerized by its alluring rhythms. "I loved it immediately," Georgia O'Keeffe recalled after her 1917 visit to New Mexico. "From then on I was always on my way back."

Artists in the Southwest struggle to come to grips with the region's grip on their imaginations: "What is it then that holds us to this curious, raw, new, old and savage land?" asks one writer. "It is not love, for the land itself is too aloof for love....The land's alive. It has a tensile strength ...a thrusting power....This it is that holds us...."

Many years after his sojourn in the Southwest, as an official artist for the U.S. government, John Mix Stanley (1814 – 1872) synthesized his vivid, romantic recollections of the region in his fantastic panorama *Chain of Spires Along the Gila River*. Accurately portraying the junction of Arizona's Gila and Colorado rivers, he exuberantly populated the landscape with cacti and animals from the farthest reaches of the desert—and his imagination. The effect is the "desert paradise" whose boundless promise so enthralled Stanley.

Traveling during the Mexican War of 1846 with General Kearny's expedition of occupation as it swept across the desert, destined for the Pacific coast, Stanley was one of the earliest Anglo-American artists to record the wonders of the

ALYCE FRANK. Morada by Mabel Dodge House, 1989, Oil on linen, 30 x 40 inches

LOUIS AKIN, *Mesa and Desert*, 1905, Oil on canvas, 30 x 36 inches

JOHN MIX STANLEY, Chain of Spires Along the Gila River, 1855, Oil on canvas, 31 x 42 inches

Southwest. Charged with the mission to accurately record the land, its flora, and its fauna, he later elaborated on his straightforward illustrations to create highly charged, exotic vistas in "stunningly beautiful fashion."

Stanley was not unique among artists of the "Great Reconnaissance," as the government's decades-long, collective exploration of its new territories was known. The scientific objectivity of artists working in the field was frequently overwhelmed by the astonishing sights that greeted them; the artists responded with romanticized interpretations that were accepted as accurate records.

To convey the profound, subjective reality that the Southwest landscape reveals to the careful observer, many artists after Stanley have found their voice in surrealist-inspired images. Moving to Taos in 1939 from New York City, where he had taught commercial art courses such as "Applied Surrealism," Thomas Benrimo (1887–1958) wed his surrealistic ideas to the unearthly beauty of the high desert and the towering mountains that sheltered the village. In painting, he believed, subjective fusions of "feeling and form are all." His imaginary, intricate landscapes, such as *White Moon Number Two*, blend internal and external landscapes in eerily elegant compositions.

A leader of the European surrealist movement, Max Ernst (1891–1976) lived in Sedona, Arizona, in the 1940s, attracted by the landscape whose colorful palette was keyed to his artistic philosophy. His "emblematic" *Colline Inspiree* is a heat-struck evocation of the bizarre, scarlet terrain.

Moody, poetic Marsden Hartley (1877–1943) went to New Mexico in 1918, traveling as a self-proclaimed "American discovering America." Permanently adrift in the world, Hartley roamed from place to place, seeking inspiration and fulfillment. He was both fascinated and repelled by Taos Mountain's ominous, looming presence: "The mountain calls for courage on the part of those who are fated to live with it." His intense identification with the mountain's "profound loneliness" gives his mountain paintings the haunting quality of symbolist self-portraits.

Like Stanley, Hartley distorted the landscape in his painted memories of New Mexico, bending it to conform to his subjective recollections. His fascination with mountains as dwellings of the gods and with the drama of death symbolized in the area's Catholic rituals—the subjects of his strangely tortured memories—are fused in *Cemetery New Mexico*. For Hartley, Stanley's idyllic "desert paradise" did not exist.

Before moving to Taos in 1934, Rebecca Salsbury James (1891–1968) absorbed many exciting avant-garde theories advanced by the artists of the famous "circle" of photographer-philosopher Alfred Stieglitz in New York City. At the urging of Stieglitz and her husband, photographer Paul Strand, a leading member of the circle, James taught herself to draw and paint.

Working one summer with Georgia O'Keeffe (1887–1986) at the Stieglitz compound in Lake George, New York, the neophyte artist adopted O'Keeffe's practice of using a pane of glass as a palette. One day James turned her glass over before wiping off the paint and noticed the luminosity of the paint seen through the glass. Thinking "something beautiful and different" could be done in the medium, she mastered reverse oil painting on glass. This extremely demanding folk-art form had also been attempted by Marsden Hartley, who later confessed to James that trying it "nearly killed" him.

In 1929 James and O'Keeffe accepted an invitation from Mabel Dodge Luhan to visit her in Taos. Recalling her own

decision to go to New Mexico, Luhan, a transplanted New York City socialite, had written, "My life broke in two right then, and I entered into the second half, a new world that replaced all the ways I had known...more strange and terrible and sweet than any I had ever been able to imagine." Luhan could have been speaking for the two artists, who blossomed in the desert. After their summer together, spent roaming the high plateaus and mountains of northern New Mexico and Arizona, Rebecca James reported that, in the "brilliant sunlight, the enchanted air," everything was "perfect." O'Keeffe experienced for the first time a sensation of "completeness" in her life and work. Both women returned to New Mexico every year after that fateful summer and ultimately abandoned their eastern existences for new lives in the space and light of the Southwest.

In *Earth and Water*, her surrealist, symbolic landscape, James layered physical and psychic elements: the prominent shell echoes the sighs of long-ago seas that once washed over the desert floor where the parched tree now thirsts, bereft of life, beneath a brilliant, indifferent blue sky.

In her paintings, O'Keeffe intuitively distilled the essence of human reality, giving it symbolic form. To her, this was the obvious approach; what else could art be about? "I often painted fragments of things because it seemed to make my statement as well as or better than the whole could.... I had to create an equivalent for what I felt about what I was looking at—not copy it." For O'Keeffe, the particular was a powerful expression of the universal. Attuned to "the unexplainable thing in nature that makes me feel the world is big far beyond my understanding," she tried to "find the feeling of infinity on the horizon line of just over the next hill." The juxtaposition in *Red Hills and Bones* of the huge spine bone and barren, spiny hills—desert artifacts usually

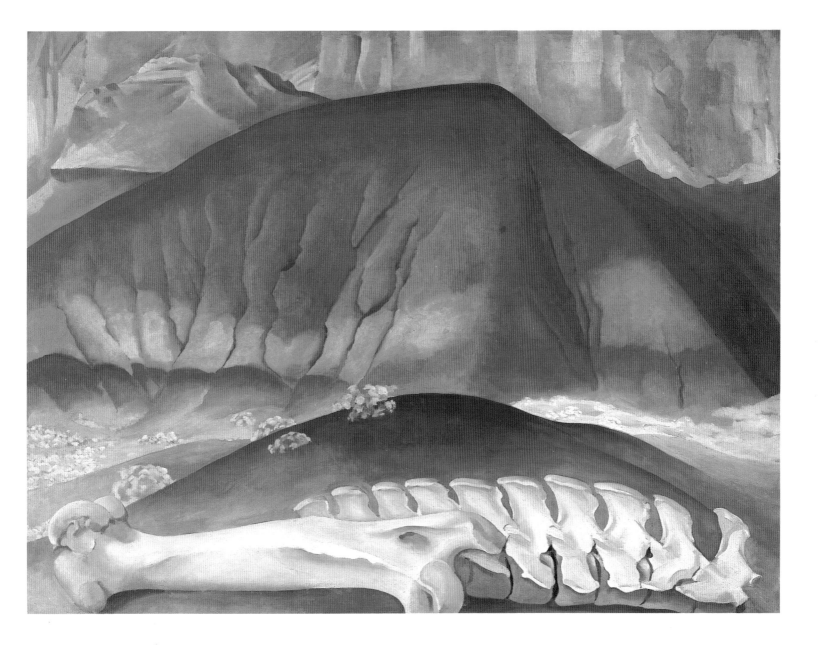

GEORGIA O'KEEFFE, Red Hills and Bones, 1941, Oil on canvas, 30 x 40 inches

MARSDEN HARTLEY, Cemetery New Mexico, 1922 – 24, Oil on canvas, 31⅝ x 39¼ inches

so commonplace as to be rendered invisible — in this altered scale are transformed into icons of the desert. By forcing the viewer to "take time to look at what I saw," the humble becomes heraldic: "When I found the beautiful white bones on the desert I picked them up and took them home.... I have used these things to say what is to me the wideness and wonder of the world...."

With her genius for selection, O'Keeffe symbolized the immanence of Hispanic religion in her simple *Black Cross, New Mexico.* "I saw the crosses so often — and often in unexpected places," she recalled, "like a thin dark veil of the Catholic Church spread over the New Mexico landscape." Pushing forward to fill the painting, the cross ominously obscures the landscape, leaving no question of its cultural and spiritual ascendance.

The ancient Catholicism that seems to grow directly from the earth, in its adobe churches and wooden crosses, overlays religions even more ancient: the nature-based worship of American Indians whose tenancy of the land was of a duration older than time when they greeted invading Spaniards, and entered history, five hundred years ago. Rumors of cities of gold far to the north fueled the Spaniards' feverish forays into the Southwest, seeking wealth similar to the Aztec splendor they had already plundered in New Spain (now Mexico).

The dismayed Spaniards soon learned that the fabled "Seven Cities of Cibola" were nothing more than Indian pueblos of adobe mud mixed with golden straw that glistened in the late afternoon sun. Their *entrada* harvested not gold but apocalyptic catastrophes sufficient to discourage even the most tenacious soul. But, amidst the relentless travails of famine, pestilence, drought, and massacre, they succumbed to the land's smiting beauty; they remained, adapting through the centuries to the rhythms of the landscape, living in symbiotic harmony with the Indians.

GEORGIA O'KEEFFE, Black Cross, New Mexico 1929
Oil on canvas, 39 x 30⅜ inches

Steeped in romantic artistic traditions of the time, British-born painter Thomas Moran (1837 – 1926) viewed the southwestern landscape differently than had the early Spaniards; he discovered pure gold waiting there for any artist capable of mining it. Vowing to "paint as an American, on an American basis, and American only," and insistent that American artists should be "true to [their] own country, in the interpretation of that beautiful and glorious scenery with which nature has so lavishly endowed our land," he exhorted artists to take advantage of "the unlimited field for the exercise of their talents to be found in this enchanting southwestern country...."

In 1873 Moran traveled with Major John Wesley Powell on his geological survey of the Grand Canyon and Colorado River. Standing at the canyon's rim, the artist gazed upon "by far the most awfully grand and impressive scene that I have ever yet seen." Painting at the site his friend Powell had designated "the greatest point of view in the Grand Canyon," Moran orchestrated a baroque paean to the chasm, composed of dramatic crescendos and fugues featuring atmospheric effects on its grotesque boulders and crevices. When Powell saw Moran's composite painting *Chasm of the Colorado,* inspired by sketches, photographs, and the artist's memory, he lauded the work for its accuracy and honesty, declaring that the artist had "represented the depths and magnitudes and distances and forms and color and clouds with the greatest fidelity" and, even more important, had gone beyond the truth to display "the beauty of the truth."

Through the years, Moran returned many times to paint the Grand Canyon, frequently as a guest of the Santa Fe Railway. Anticipating the new age of the twentieth century, the ambitious railway had blazed a trail to the Pacific coast, its steel tracks cutting through the Southwest desert. However much it was the vanguard of westward-bound, industrial America, a key part of the railway's appeal was the access it gave disillusioned Easterners to the pristine, exotic Southwest landscape and indigenous people untouched by the ravages of the twentieth century. Railroad officials launched a visionary promotional campaign, engaging prominent artists to paint the wonders of the "Santa Fe Southwest" for posters, calendars, menus, and brochures. Soon, the SFRR logo — a loco-

THOMAS MORAN. Chasm of the Colorado, 1873 – 74, Oil on canvas, 84¾ x 144¾ inches

motive wheel encircling a cross — decorated art reproductions distributed throughout the country.

Flamboyant journalist and promoter Charles Lummis, celebrated for his intense Americanism (he coined the slogan, "See America First!"), inadvertently helped the railway recruit talented artists for its ambitious publicity campaign when he exhorted them to paint the Southwest: "Any man who is really an artist," he declared, "will find the Southwest . . . a region where the ingenuity, the imagination, and the love of God are . . . visible at every turn. . . . It is high time for the artists to come upon the Southwest."

Lummis himself had "come upon the Southwest" in 1892, walking from Ohio to Los Angeles along the Santa Fe Trail on a self-proclaimed trek of discovery and conquest that prompted him to exclaim, "My name is Lummis, I'm the West!" The stampede of artists eager to explore and exploit this newly discovered, quintessentially American territory was on.

The SFRR's steady patronage and the artists' enduring fascination with the canyon's grandiose vistas led several artists to devote their attention to the Grand Canyon almost exclusively. To produce his gorgeous paintings, William Robinson Leigh (1866 – 1955) literally immersed himself "in the chasm, surrounded by its pinnacled glory." In 1909 Leigh confided to his journal, "Though I am perched far out on this naked tongue of rock where any wandering current of air would surely find me, though I huddle as closely under my sketching umbrella as I can, yet the perspiration trickles from my elbow. And this, let me add, means something in this dry atmosphere." No sacrifice was too great in pursuit of homage worthy of the canyon.

Gunnar Widforss (1879 – 1934) spent his mature years painting the Grand Canyon, from both its rim and its floor;

he was obsessed with conveying its enormous depths. After his death at the canyon, a peak was named Widforss Point in his honor.

While the Grand Canyon was source and inspiration for many paintings in the SFRR collection, most of the artists who created these and other works of art for the collection lived not in Arizona but in the remote mountain art colonies of Taos and Santa Fe, in northern New Mexico. Like the Seven Cities of Cibola, these two small villages glowed in the light of the vivid tales told by itinerant artists who had passed through, lingering just long enough to complete commissions for magazines and the federal government — and to fall under the area's spell.

In 1849 Richard Kern painted what probably is the earliest artistic rendering of Taos Valley, long before its namesake village — crouched at the foot of majestic Taos Mountain — became the famous art colony. An official artist with Fremont's expedition sent to search for a railroad route to the Pacific along the 35th parallel, Kern had been stranded in New Mexico for several months, having survived a tragic winter with Fremont's party in the impassable, frozen mountains of northern New Mexico, where many others died and cannibalism was rumored. Before joining a punitive expedition against the Navajos later that year and heading west, the artist sketched numerous scenes in northern New Mexico. However, it was not Kern's work that inspired artists to seek the wonders of Taos.

The story of the founding of the Taos art colony has taken on the aura of a creation myth. As the oft-told tale goes, in the summer of 1898 two young artists, Ernest L. Blumenschein (1874 – 1960) and Bert Phillips (1868 – 1956), outfitted with a horse and wagon in Denver and set out on a sketching trip down the crest of the southern Rockies, into Mexico. In Paris,

several years earlier, the young men had been fascinated by the reminiscences of fellow artist Joseph Henry Sharp (1859–1953). Now considered the father of the Taos art colony, Sharp had spent the summer of 1893 there, writing and illustrating "The Harvest Dance of the Pueblo Indians of New Mexico" for *Harper's Weekly*. Sharp had traveled extensively throughout the West, recording the traditional Indian life he feared was threatened by the onslaught of westward migration. But no other locale affected him as did the magical Taos Valley.

His enthusiasm was contagious; it infected the young artists, whose excitement at the prospect of their adventure was equaled only by their "woeful ignorance" of horses and wagons, and of the rugged terrain and harsh climate they would encounter on their wilderness pilgrimage. On September 4, 1898, as they reached the summit of the 12,000-foot-high La Veta Pass and entered New Mexico, they noticed "a decided change in the scenery" and a dramatic deterioration in road conditions. Rounding a narrow curve during a thunderstorm, their wagon slid off the slippery road, coming to rest in a precarious tilt over a steep canyon. A wagon wheel was broken. FATE had intervened. The toss of a coin sent Blumenschein down the mountain into Taos on horseback, carrying the broken wheel to have it repaired.

The young midwesterner was unprepared for the landscape he passed through on "the most impressive journey of [his] life." When he sighted Taos in the distance across twenty miles of "great lakes of sagebrush," a landscape unlike any he had ever seen met his eyes: "...Sharp had not painted for me the land or the mountains and plains and clouds. No artist had ever recorded the New Mexico I was now seeing....My destiny was being decided....I was getting my own impressions from nature, seeing it for the first time with my own eyes, uninfluenced by the art of any man." For the two artists, "it had to end in the Taos valley."

Blumenschein lingered in Taos only a few months before returning to Paris; Phillips remained there until his death, devoting himself to lyrical paintings of Taos Indians. *Song of the Aspen* is Phillips's rapturous ode to the beauty he found in Indian ritual and song, performed in the serene forest that to the painter expressed "spiritual messages."

Beginning in 1902 Sharp returned every summer to paint the Indians, his ethnological intentions modified by his response to the romance of their rituals. *Sunset Dance—*

Ceremony to the Evening Sun is perhaps his finest painting. It evokes Sharp's primary concerns: colorful costumes; communal ceremonies; the soft evening sunset symbolizing a dying race; and, above all, the sheer beauty of the imposing mountain backdrop.

Over the next several years, artists with similar academic backgrounds and romantic concerns joined Sharp and Phillips in Taos. In 1915 six art colonists: Sharp, Blumenschein, Phillips, William Herbert "Buck" Dunton (1878–1936), Oscar Berninghaus (1874–1952), and Eanger Irving Couse (1866–1936) organized the Taos Society of Artists (TSA), primarily to market their work through national touring exhibitions. The TSA was an instant sensation; it literally put Taos on the international art map and provided enough income for most of the artists to allow them to remain in Taos to work as fine artists.

By the time the TSA disbanded in 1927 (having served its purpose so well it no longer was needed), its eleven active members included Walter Ufer (1876–1936), who abandoned his studio in Taos to work directly in the brilliant sunlight that illuminates his paintings, and Victor Higgins (1884–1949), whose explorations in modernist techniques and perspectives forcefully revealed the powerful elements of the Southwest landscape and set him apart from his more conservative TSA colleagues.

While legends surrounding the Taos art colony conjure up images of rugged men who captured the landscape, paintbrushes in hand, many talented women artists also found in Taos "something more than the place of [their] fondest dreams." One of the earliest to settle there was Ila McAfee (b. 1897), who arrived in 1925. Noted for her paintings of horses, McAfee was also attracted to the exotic wildlife that ranged freely in the rugged landscape.

ILA MCAFEE, Antelope, n.d., Oil on canvas, 39½ x 45½ inches

By the late teens, these academically trained artists were joined by modernists seeking much the same inspiration for their stylistic experiments, brought to Taos, for the most part, by Mabel Dodge Luhan. Called to New Mexico in 1917 by her third husband, Maurice Sterne, Mabel initially had no intention of remaining there. Bored with Sterne after only a few weeks of marriage, she exiled him, explaining, "I'm going to send you out to the Southwest. I've heard there are wonderful things to paint. Indians."

Soon after he arrived in Santa Fe, the disconsolate Sterne sent a letter urging her to travel to New Mexico to "save the Indians, their art—culture—reveal it to the world!" Coincidentally, Mabel had visited a medium who predicted that her life would be devoted to helping the Indians and in turn being guided by one. This mystic conjunction was sufficiently potent to send Mabel west.

Disdainful of the "trite" Santa Fe art scene Maurice introduced her to, she impulsively left for the remote northern village of Taos. Arriving late at night after an arduous car trip over primitive roads, she made the instantaneous and irrevocable decision to settle in Taos, sight unseen. It wasn't long before she discarded Sterne to marry handsome, silent Tony Luhan, the Taos Indian who became her fourth and final husband.

Mabel's voice in this utopian wilderness called to artists, writers, celebrities, and eccentrics she had left behind in New York. One of her earliest guests was Andrew Dasburg (1887–1979), the young modernist artist who had studied at the Art Students League, visited Gertrude Stein in Paris, and exhibited in the 1913 Armory Show. Cézanne's influence permeates Dasburg's New Mexico paintings; settling there permanently, he in turn influenced other modernist artists through the example of his work and in his role of teacher

and mentor.

Another of Mabel's guests—the major American modernist John Marin (1870–1953)—left behind a distinctive stylistic legacy after his two summer visits in 1929 and 1930. Making more than one hundred watercolors, Marin vignetted his scenes—frequently portraits of mountains—framing the semiabstract compositions to intensify their effect. Marin had forecast his positive response to the Taos area a year before his first trip there: "the true artists must perforce go from time to time to the elemental big forms—Sky, Sea, Mountains...." In truth, the big forms intimidated Marin; he wrote to Stieglitz of the inhuman landscape, where people were completely insignificant—except the Indians, who communed intimately with the earth in their rhythmic dances. So moved was he by the awesome spectacle of the corn dance, depicted in *Dance of the Santo Domingo Indians,* that

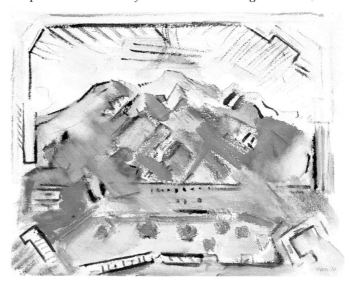

JOHN MARIN, Near Taos, New Mexico, 1930
Watercolor on paper, 16¾ x 21½ inches

Ernest L. Blumenschein, *Sangre de Cristo Mountains*, 1925, Oil on canvas, 50¼ x 60 inches

he compared attempts to paint it to "rewriting Bach."

While most of the academically trained TSA artists resisted change, Ernest Blumenschein occasionally joined Victor Higgins to explore the modernist trends that arrived with the steady stream of avant-garde artists who visited Luhan. Blumenschein's vivid portrayal of the Holy Week procession trudging through the snow toward the voluptuous mountains in *Sangre de Cristo Mountains* distills the crucial link between culture and nature. In this symbolic reenactment of Christ's crucifixion, the earthen village mediates between worshipping pilgrims and the sheltering mountain that represents — *becomes* — the firmament of heaven. Not merely a backdrop for human activities, the mountain is the material for their shelter, which in turn echoes the volume and silhouette of the mountain in whose arms it is held.

Seventy miles to the south, in Santa Fe, an art colony flourished around an art museum built to attract artists to the community and to support their careers once they arrived. In 1916, during the museum's construction, director Edgar Hewett met the leading New York social-realist artist Robert Henri (1865 – 1929) and invited him to Santa Fe. A few months later he renewed his invitation, writing, "before things get much farther along I am tremendously anxious to have the ideal in Art that you stand for brought into the ken of our people."

Gerald Cassidy (1869 – 1934), one of the artists who enjoyed Hewett's patronage, had been recommended to him as a man who "never drinks, chews, or smokes, is a free thinker, and of a very poetic temperament." *Cui Bono?*, considered Cassidy's masterpiece, was first exhibited at San Diego's Panama-California Exposition in 1915. The phrase "cui bono" is described as "a pretentious substitute for To what end? or What is the good?" Cassidy intended the

GERALD CASSIDY, Cui Bono?, c. 1911
Oil on canvas, 93½ x 48 inches

21

title — and the large painting — to reinforce the notion of Indian as noble Roman, right down to the Romanesque toga. In this portrait, the composed, idealized Indian is a mythical personage, symbol of a civilized race of peaceful farmers living in a community whose roots reach into the soil, beyond the beginning of time.

In the 1920s Mabel Luhan and writer Mary Austin, who had moved to Santa Fe from California to focus her social activism on regional issues, converged upon the plight of New Mexico's Indians, who were plagued and harassed by greedy profiteers and politicians who wanted to take their land and forcibly assimilate their children into mainstream American society. Cassidy and several other artists joined the crusaders; they naturally sympathized with the Indian "as a human being."

Himself an activist and author of the influential book *The Art Spirit,* Henri accepted Hewett's invitation to visit Santa Fe. He was curious about its suitability as a regular summer retreat and hoped to encounter "whatever of the great spirit there is in the Southwest." His enthusiastic accounts of the glorious summer season in the rarefied, crystal-clear climate of the mountain village and his sumptuous portraits of Indians and Hispanic subjects painted in bright hues persuaded well-known artists George Bellows (1882 – 1925),

VELINO SHIJE HERRERA (MA-PE-WI), Buffalo Hunt, c. 1930, Watercolor on paper, 25 x 29 ½ inches

Leon Kroll (1884–1974), Paul Burlin (1886–1969), and John Sloan (1871–1951) to visit.

Bellows spent a pleasant month painting the "strange and stimulating countryside" and the fascinating Indian pueblos. However, toward the end of his stay, when he exhibited his paintings at the museum, a local critic ridiculed "Bellows' Green Cow," a derisive reference to his modernist sensibility. The insulted artist never returned.

A former newspaper artist, Sloan had studied with Henri in New York and was a member of The Eight, also known as the Ashcan School. He and his wife Dolly drove to Santa Fe in 1919, establishing a summer home where he returned every summer for thirty-one years. His warmth, humor, and love of the local color enliven his affectionate portraits of community life. One can almost hear the melody in his *Music in the Plaza,* a festive community gathering in the soft evening atmosphere on the revered plaza—the heart of the ancient town, established by Spaniards in 1610. In the 1920s, when this painting was completed, Santa Fe's charming customs were still very much in the Spanish tradition.

Sloan also championed the art of the Pueblo Indians, such as that of Velino Shije Herrera (Ma-Pe-Wi), whose *Buffalo Hunt* exhibits the "primitive directness and strength" and the "sophistication and subtlety" that Sloan claimed were evidence

PABLITA VELARDE, Rooster Pull, c. 1953–55, Gouache on paper, 20 x 31 inches

of a modernist sensibility.

Sloan's friends Stuart Davis (1894–1964) and Edward Hopper (1882–1967) did not respond as warmly to the quaint place. Hopper visited only once, in 1925. Finding little that interested him, he preoccupied himself with compositions featuring angular shapes in severe sunlight. Davis complained that the New Mexico landscape was so assertive that it was impossible for the artist to assert his will upon it. Not content to "merely record" the landscape, Davis was defeated; he framed his renderings in borders resembling those around snapshots in family albums, telling commentary on his feeling that in the Southwest his status had been diminished from visitor to that of tourist.

Decades later, in a visual souvenir of his summer drive through the state, the contemporary California artist David Hockney (b. 1937) juxtaposed popular tourist sites in northern Arizona in a montage of images held together by a winding two-lane highway that disappears somewhere in Monument Valley. Like Davis's New Mexico paintings, Hockney's *Arizona* mimics the superficiality of tourist photos — and experiences.

Despite Bellows' rude reception by Santa Fe's art mavens, modernism was not a stranger to the art colony. In the early 1920s five young artists, perhaps rebelling against the elitist members of the Taos Society of Artists, formed their own group, Los Cinco Pintores. The painters were united by their common interest in advancing their careers more than by their individual styles.

Bakós (1891–1977) and Willard Nash (1898–1943) embraced modernist influences, particularly cubist volumes and distortion, and a fauvist emphasis on expressive palettes of "great brilliance." Unlike the TSA artists, these young men had not studied in Europe. They were free of academy- and self-imposed constraints on freewheeling experimentation. Uncertain quite how to respond, one critic found "freshness" in Nash's work that was "very pleasing." One cannot quarrel with this assessment, but Nash's work was more than pleasing; his modernist sensibility, as is forcefully apparent in *Sun Mountain Abstract*, was sophisticated and successful.

The era ended by the Great Depression was in retrospect idyllic and innocent. In the harsh light of the natural and political disasters that befell most Americans in the 1930s, the atmosphere revealed grim aspects. Artists who once had painted their native neighbors in bucolic settings performing ritual acts now took a harder look to portray their struggles and suffering.

Kenneth Adams (1897–1981), the youngest member of the Taos Society of Artists, had studied at the Art Institute of Chicago and with Andrew Dasburg in Woodstock, New York. After Dasburg persuaded him to move to New Mexico, his empathy with Hispanics became a central theme in his art. *The Dry Ditch*, painted years later, powerfully conveys both the grim impact of the Depression on agrarian New Mexicans and influences on the artist of the social realism portrayed by radical Mexican muralists during that era.

Barbara Latham's portrayal of Taos in *Tourist Town, Taos* is, on the surface, a colorful view of a lazy Saturday afternoon with an exotic twist. A deeper reading of the scene reveals Latham's piercing criticism of the degradation of Indians caused by the intrusion of "civilization" into the timeless tranquility of their lives. In the scene, tourists costumed as cowboys and cowgirls parade around the town plaza, oblivious of the shrouded Indians languishing near their wagon, surrounded by automobiles — harbingers of impending social crisis, as old virtues are replaced by modern vices. The signs visible on the buildings reinforce Latham's view

BARBARA LATHAM, Tourist Town, Taos, 1940 – 49, Egg tempera on masonite, 24 x 35¾ inches

HENRIETTE WYETH, Doña Nestorita, 1940
Oil on canvas, 46 x 37 inches

of corrupting influences in the community; they read: bar, liquor, drugs — all anathemas to traditional Indian culture.

Other artists addressed the underlying tensions aggravated by political, religious, and cultural differences in communities that had enjoyed undisturbed equilibrium for centuries. Texas artist Alexandre Hogue (b. 1898) is best known for his Depression-era paintings, but his paintings of Pueblo culture in transition reveal his interest in their spiritual dilemma. In *Procession of the Saint — Santo Domingo,* the priest — his eyes obscured by dark glasses, a stubby cigar hovering over his ample belly — turns his back on the ritual and, by implication, on the Indians, while indulging in sensuous pleasures alien to their sensibilities.

After World War II, artists migrated in growing numbers to the Southwest, lured in part by art schools that accepted veterans supported by the GI Bill. By 1951 there were so many working artists in New Mexico that the museum in Santa Fe was forced to end its open-door exhibition policy. Following the announcement that its next annual show would be juried, John Sloan, ill in New York, sent a frantic telegram to his friend and fellow artist, Will Shuster. It read: "I have just heard that S. F. Art Museum is having its first Juried Ex. — STOP! This means there will be no more distinction about the Annual Ex. STOP. The famous Open Door Annual of Santa Fe will be no more. STOP.... And watch the miserable, puny, stinking, pallid efforts to show twentieth class imitations of the current fashions. OH STOP!" A few days later he died.

Sloan's death marked the passing of an era. The heyday of the remote art colonies was past. But Southwest art enjoyed a new vigor as the former colonies became vital communities whose museums, college and university art departments, private art schools, galleries, and art publications offered support and encouragement to the growing population of artists.

The artistic heritage of the last century has provided today's painters of the Southwest a wealth of material. Today's artists draw not only upon the art made by indigenous peoples during the tranquil epoch before the Americans came, but from the innocent years before World War I, the giddy, adventurous twenties; the idealistic, social-realistic Depression years; the bland, modernist fifties.

After the tumultuous sixties turned art on its head, modernism exploded into a postmodern profusion that thrives in the Southwest. Diversity best describes the work of contemporary painters, who choose to — but probably could not do otherwise — cast their fates in the Southwest, far from

MARIA BACA, Paisaje en Verano, 1991, Oil on canvas, 66 x 72 inches

KENNETH MILLER ADAMS, The Dry Ditch, 1964
Oil on canvas, 50 x 36 inches

major art centers but close to the source of their inspiration.

In *Processing Sheep*, Willard Midgette (1937–1978) transcends the painting's realistic facade by rendering the scene life-size; the immediacy of the image has a psychological impact on the viewer, who becomes a vicarious participant in his encounter with contemporary American Indians in the Southwest landscape. The traditional Indian shepherd has become a thoroughly modern "processor."

Like Midgette, Woody Gwyn (b. 1944) paints in a large format to bring the viewer into the landscape. In *Highway and Mesa*, serene, sacred Black Mesa—the timeless, spiritually charged landmark in northern New Mexico—becomes just another roadside attraction, a split-second sensation glimpsed by speeding motorists traversing the vast Southwest desert.

Best known for her portraits and still lifes, Henriette Wyeth (b. 1907) and her husband, painter Peter Hurd (1904–1984), staked their artistic claim in the Hondo Valley of southern New Mexico, near Hurd's birthplace in Roswell and far from the art colonies in the north. In her portrait *Doña Nestorita*, Wyeth was compelled to place the Hispanic elder in the landscape that had so significantly shaped her spirit.

Maria Baca (b. 1951), like other contemporary Hispanic artists, is unwilling to remain simply subject matter for Anglo artists. She portrays Hispanic culture—her culture—through her own eyes; her dreams and memories of family and community transcend the particular to become larger statements of the human condition.

The "spirit of place" that first lured artists to the fabled Southwest still holds them in its spell: they still are captivated by its blue skies, red earth, pungent rituals, and ethereal space and light.

The mystique retains its allure; the Southwest remains the significant "Other" in the American imagination.

WILLARD MIDGETTE. Processing Sheep, 1976, Oil on linen, 108¼ x 156½ inches

THERE MUST HAVE BEEN AN IMMENSE APPEAL
in the caves for their highness, the unstinted reach of vision, the sense
of cuddling safety against the mother rock....How comfortably they must
have snuggled together around the three-cornered fireplaces when
the torrent of the rain came falling like a silver curtain between them
and the world, or the wolfish wind howled and scraped against the
retaining wall!

MARY AUSTIN, *The Land of Journey's Ending,* 1924

JULES TAVERNIER, Indian Village of Acoma, 1879, Oil on canvas, 64 x 29½ inches

WILLIAM HENRY HOLMES, Cliff House in 1875, 1875, Watercolor on paper, 9⅞ x 13½ inches

OSCAR E. BERNINGHAUS, A Showery Day, Grand Canyon, 1915, Oil on canvas, 30 x 40 inches

THE ROCK...

has a more fiery hue than usual, as if it
were glowing red hot. I think an egg would
fry beautifully on it....The fierce light
dazzles....Suddenly the peak I have been
painting is plunged in shadow...Above Point
Yuma the vanguards of a storm are hurrying
up the sky....I gather up my belongings
and retire to the shelter of an overhanging
ledge of rocks where...I stretch myself
upon the ground and scornfully bid the
giant do his worst.

WILLIAM ROBINSON LEIGH

WILLIAM ROBINSON LEIGH, Grand Canyon, 1911, Oil on canvas, 28 x 34 inches

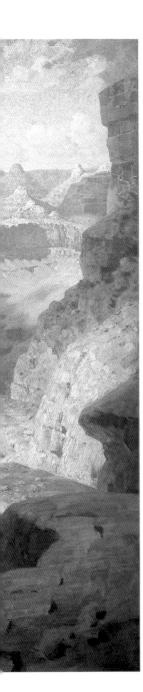

THOUGH I AM PERCHED FAR OUT

on this naked tongue of rock where any wandering current of air would surely find me,

though I huddle as closely under my sketching umbrella as I can, yet the perspiration

trickles from my elbow. And this, let me add, means something in this dry atmosphere....

Some of my colors are melting and only by judicious tilting of the palette are

prevented from sliding off.

WILLIAM ROBINSON LEIGH

WILLIAM ROBINSON LEIGH, Grand Canyon, 1911, Oil on canvas, 66 x 99 inches

SUDDENLY A DEEP VOICE,

vibrant with suppressed emotion, spoke from behind me into my left ear:
"Do you not think that all life comes from the mountain?" An elderly Indian had come
up to me, inaudible in his moccasins, and had asked me this heaven knows how far-reaching
question.... Obviously all life came from the mountain, for where there is water, there
is life. Nothing could be more obvious. In his question, I felt a swelling emotion
connected with the word "mountain." I replied, "Everyone can see
that you speak the truth."

CARL JUNG, *Memories, Dreams, Reflections,* 1963

WALTER UFER, Where the Desert Meets the Mountain, 1922, Oil on canvas, 36½ x 40¼ inches

JÓZEF G. BAKÓS. El Sanctuário, Chimayó, before 1940, Oil on canvas, 30 x 34 inches

GEORGE WESLEY BELLOWS, *Pueblo, Tesuque, Number One*, 1917, Oil on canvas, 34 x 44 inches

I'M in love with Santa Fe;   How the folks who aren't in it,
Like it better every day;   Ever stand it, any way,
But I wonder, every minute,   Not to be in Santa Fe.

MAE PEREGRINE, *Santa Fe*, 1915

LEON KROLL. Santa Fe Hills, 1917, Oil on canvas, 34 x 40¼ inches   WILLARD NASH. Landscape, c. 1920s, Oil on canvas, 23¼ x 29½ inches

On sunday evenings when the band played,
youths would stream in one direction round the Plaza and in the opposite direction
maidens, just as apart from one another and just as aware of one another as I have seen
them in Mexican cities. Older women moved nunlike...with soft black shawls
over their heads, the fringe hanging down their dresses.

Witter Bynner, *Selected Poems,* 1936

John Sloan, Music in the Plaza, 1920, Oil on canvas, 26 x 32 inches

44   JOHN SLOAN. East At Sunset, 1921, Oil on canvas, 26 x 32 inches

JOHN SLOAN. *Chama Running Red*, 1927, Oil on canvas, 30 x 40 inches

46   WILLIAM HERBERT "BUCK" DUNTON, Sunset in the Foothills, Oil on canvas, 40 x 50 inches

THE WEST HAS PASSED—MORE'S THE PITY.

In another twenty-five years the old-time westerner will have gone, too—gone with the

buffalo and the antelope. I'm going to hand down to posterity a bit of unadulterated

real thing, if it's the last thing I do—and I'm going to do it *muy pronto*.

WILLIAM HERBERT "BUCK" DUNTON, *Pioneer Artists of Taos*, 1955

WILLIAM HERBERT "BUCK" DUNTON, The Cattlebuyer, 1922, Oil on canvas, 50 x 60 inches   47

DESERT: LUMINOUS, FOSSILIZED NETWORK
of an inhuman intelligence, of a radical indifference — the indifference not merely
of the sky, but of the geological undulations, where the metaphysical passions of space and
time alone crystallize. Here the terms of desire are turned upside down each day,
and night annihilates them. But wait for the dawn to rise, with the awakening of
the fossil sounds, the animal silence.

JEAN BAUDRILLARD, *America*, 1986

IN THE HOUR OF THE GREY DESERT'S SPLENDOR,
it is good to be among the Rio Grande dunes down by the Border.
Across their spherical curves, the sharp shadows grow long.... Aloft in the solitude of the
firmament move high bronze clouds.... In the mystery of twilight, poetic softness veils
the desolation, and coolness comes with velvet touch.... All shadows, all reflections have
gone, only the west remains luminous green and silver.

ROSS CALVIN, *Sky Determines: An Interpretation of the Southwest,* 1948

MARSDEN HARTLEY, Desert Scene, c. 1922, Oil on board, 25¾ x 31⅞ inches

OVER the rounded sides of the Rockies, the
    aspens of autumn,
The aspens of autumn
Like yellow hair of a tigress brindled with pine.

D. H. LAWRENCE, *Autumn at Taos,* 1922

SHELDON PARSONS, Santa Fe Mountains in October, c. 1919 – 22
Oil on plywood, 36 x 24 inches

AS I VISIT THEIR VILLAGES
and talk with my Indian friends, I see and hear the
young bucks wrapped in their white blankets standing
on the bridge singing a love song in the
moonlight, and I feel the romance of youth....
I believe that it is the romance of this great
pure-aired land that makes the most
lasting impression on my mind and heart.

BERT GEER PHILLIPS,

BERT GEER PHILLIPS, Song of the Aspen, c. 1926 – 28
Oil on canvas, 40 x 27 inches

THEY wear squash-flowers cut in silver
And carve the sun on canyon walls;
Their words are born of storm and calyx,
Eagles, and waterfalls.

They weave the thunder in the basket,
And paint the lightning in the bowl;
Taking the village to the rainbow,
And the rainbow to the soul.

HANIEL LONG, *Indians*

GUNNAR WIDFORSS, Phantom Ranch, Grand Canyon, 1925, Watercolor on paper, 21 x 24 inches

ERNEST L. BLUMENSCHEIN. The Lake, n.d., Oil on canvas, 24⅛ x 27 inches

THE GRAND CANYON IS NOT A SOLITUDE.
It is a living, moving, pulsating being, ever changing in form and color, pinnacles and
towers springing into being out of unseen depths. From dark shades of brown and black,
scarlet flames suddenly flash out and then die away into stretches of
orange and purple.... Among ... its cathedral spires, its arches and its domes,
and the deeper recesses of its inner gorge its spirit, its soul, the very spirit of the
living God himself lives and moves....

R. B. STANTON, *Grand Canyon of Arizona,* 1909

60   JOHN MARIN. Storm over Taos, 1930, Watercolor over graphite, 15 x 20⅞ inches

VICTOR HIGGINS. Spring Rain, c. 1924, Oil on canvas, 40 x 43 inches   61

MARSDEN HARTLEY, Landscape: New Mexico, 1920, Oil on composition board, 25⅝ x 29¼ inches

MARSDEN HARTLEY. Landscape No. 3, (Cash Entry Mines, New Mexico), 1920, Oil on canvas, 27¾ x 35¾ inches

IN THE WINTERTIME,

one only knows the mountain from a distance, and then one can get it whole.

One can ponder its vast bulk, and watch its changing forms and speculate upon the mysteries

it hides within its canyons and in its deep folds.... Early in the morning the

mountain looks crumpled and as though a lot of pyramids were stacked against

each other to form it...

MABEL DODGE LUHAN, *Winter in Taos,* 1935

PAUL LANTZ. Snow in Santa Fe, c. 1935, Oil on masonite, 30 x 40 inches

HOWARD COOK. Winter Mountain, Cycle No. 4, 1955, Oil on canvas, 26 x 55 inches (*opposite*)

EDWARD HOPPER, St. Francis' Towers, Santa Fe, 1925, Watercolor on paper, 13½ x 19½ inches

PETER HURD. Alamogordo Ranch, 1948, Egg tempera, 26 x 40 inches

WHAT IS NEW MEXICO, THEN?

How sum it up? It is a vast, harsh, poverty-stricken, varied, and beautiful land,
a breeder of artists and warriors.... It is primitive, undeveloped, overused, new, raw, rich
with tradition, old, and mellow. It is a land full of the essence of peace,
although its history is one of invasions and conflicts. It is itself, an entity, at times
infuriating, at times utterly delightful to its lovers, a land that draws and holds
men and women with ties that cannot be explained or submitted to reason.

OLIVER LA FARGE, *New Mexico,* 1952

THOMAS HART BENTON, New Mexico, 1926, Oil and egg tempera on board, 20¼ x 26¼ inches

E. MARTIN HENNINGS, Through the Chamisa, c. 1920s, Oil on canvas, 45 x 43 inches

OSCAR E. BERNINGHAUS, Haytime and Showers, 1940, Oil on canvas, 35 x 40 inches

DASBURG FOUND THE ENVIRONMENT CONGENIAL
and stimulating. He responded to the natural growth of the forms that met his eye
on all sides....He had from early youth the precious faculty of perceiving the organic
movement in nature and in man, and of being able to let it stream out of him onto his
canvases. His trees live and reach upward, and, as there is a peculiar vibration in
matter invisible to the eye, so there is also in his paintings of the adobe village
streets....His work is always alive and strong.

MABEL DODGE LUHAN, *Taos and its Artists,* 1947

ANDREW DASBURG, New Mexican Village, 1926, Oil on canvas, 24 x 30 inches

HOUGHTON CRANFORD SMITH, Return from the Rabbit Hunt, c. 1920s, Oil on canvas, 35⅛ x 56½ inches

MAYNARD DIXON, Desert Southwest, 1944, Oil on canvas, 40 x 36 inches (*opposite*)

I KNEW A MOUNTAIN ONCE,
over toward Lost Borders, which could both glow and pale,
pale after the burning, like a lovely neglected woman who burned
to no purpose, a dark mountain, whose bareness was like a pain.

MARY AUSTIN, *The Land of Journey's Ending*, 1924

GEORGIA O'KEEFFE, The Mountain, New Mexico, 1931, Oil on canvas, 30 x 36 inches

VICTOR HIGGINS, Mountain Forms #2, c. 1924 – 27, Oil on canvas, 40½ x 43 inches

As I came down from Cundiyo,
Upon the road to Chimayo
I met three women walking;
Each held a sorrow to her breast,
And one of them a small cross pressed—
Three black-shawled women walking.

ALICE CORBIN HENDERSON, *Cundiyo,* 1920

EMIL BISTTRAM, Church at Ranchos, c. 1930, Watercolor on paper, 13½ x 19½ inches

The ranchos de taos church

is one of the most beautiful buildings left in the United States by the early Spaniards.
Most artists who spend any time in Taos have to paint it, I suppose, just as they have to
paint a self-portrait. I had to paint it—the back of it several times, the front once.

GEORGIA O'KEEFFE, *Georgia O'Keeffe*, 1976

Fritz Scholder, Adobe Church, n.d., Oil on canvas, 68 x 80 inches

Georgia O'Keeffe, Ranchos Church, c. 1929, Oil on canvas, 24 x 36 inches (*opposite*)

I HEARD THE SINGING AND DRUMMING
as soon as we reached the Pueblo, and it drew me strongly and I left the others and
ran hurriedly towards it with my heart beating....I heard the voice of the One coming from
the Many...all of a sudden I was brought up against the tribe, where a different instinct
ruled, where a different knowledge gave a different power from any I had known....
So when I heard that great Indian chorus singing for the first time, I felt a strong
new life was present there enfolding me.

MABEL DODGE LUHAN, *Edge of Taos Desert*, 1937

JOSEPH HENRY SHARP, Sunset Dance—Ceremony to the Evening Sun, 1924, Oil on canvas, 25⅛ x 30 inches

THEN SUDDENLY THEY CAME. OUT OF THE WIDE, WHITE UNIVERSE, out of myth and legend, out of the depths of America itself. They came filing into the open plaza, shaking their gourd rattles, uttering their strange cries. A line of figures part man, part beast, part bird. Bare bodies splotched with paint, sinuously bending at the waist....They began dancing....No longer man nor beast nor bird, but embodied forces of earth and sky swirling across the sea of snow from the blue mountains on the horizon....Dancing as gods have always danced before their people.

FRANK WATERS, *Masked Gods,* 1950

JOHN MARIN, Dance of the Santo Domingo Indians, 1929, Watercolor and charcoal on paper, 22 x 30¾ inches

"SEE," OCHWIAY BIANO SAID, "HOW CRUEL THE WHITES LOOK.
Their lips are thin, their noses sharp, their faces furrowed and distorted by folds.
Their eyes have a staring expression; they are always seeking something.
What are they seeking? The whites always want something; they are always uneasy
and restless. We do not know what they want. We do not understand them.
We think that they are mad." I asked him why he thought the whites were all mad.
"They say that they think with their heads," he replied. "Why of course.
What do you think with?" I asked him in surprise. "We think here," he said,
indicating his heart.

CARL JUNG, *Memories, Dreams, Reflections,* 1963

THERE IS A VASTNESS, AN IMMENSITY, AND A PEACEFUL HUSH
of an enormous cathedral about Arizona's great canyons. Whoever has been within these
walls, and has seen the flocks of sheep and goats grazing, heard the distant tinkle
of the lead goat's bell,...must yearn to
perpetuate his impressions of those precious moments.

GERARD C. DELANO, *Artists of the Rockies and the Golden West*, 1980

ERNEST L. BLUMENSCHEIN, Afternoon of a Sheep Herder, n.d., Oil on canvas, 28 x 50 inches

91

THOMAS BENRIMO, White Moon Number Two, c. 1954, Oil on masonite, 32 x 48 inches

MAX ERNST. *Colline inspirée* (Inspired Hill), 1950, Oil on canvas, 28¾ x 36¼ inches (*opposite*)

WHAT SPLENDOR! ONLY THE TAWNY EAGLE
could really sail out into the splendor of it all.... It had a splendid silent terror,
and a vast far-and-wide magnificence which made it way beyond mere aesthetic
appreciation. Never is the light more pure and overweening than there,
arching with a royalty almost cruel over the hollow, uptilted world.

D. H. LAWRENCE, *Phoenix: The Posthumous Papers of D. H. Lawrence*, 1936

ANDREW DASBURG, New Mexico Landscape, 1932, Watercolor on paper, 19 x 22 inches

EMIL BISTTRAM, Nature Rhythms, 1958, Watercolor on paper, 18¼ x 22 inches

B. J. O. NORDFELDT, Geophysical Forms, 1954, Oil on linen, 34 x 48 inches

EVERY MESA WAS DUPLICATED BY A CLOUD MESA,
like a reflection, which lay motionless above it or moved slowly up from behind it.
These cloud formations seemed to be always there, however hot and blue the sky.
Sometimes they were flat terraces, ledges of vapour....The great tables of granite set down
in an empty plain were inconceivable without their attendant clouds, which were a
part of them, as the smoke is part of the censer, or the foam of the wave.

WILLA CATHER, *Death Comes for the Archbishop*, 1927

WITH THE BUFFALO WENT THE INDIAN AND WITH THE CATTLE
came the cowboy. Created by that northward sweep of the long-horned herds he was
briefly the dominant figure in the whole Southwest as the mountain man
had been before him and the Mexican rico before that. He was a figure as distinctive
as either of these but the period of his importance was hardly more than a generation.
It came to an end when money and fences laid hold of the grasslands.
But he survives in the imaginations of men....he is an immortal stereotype.

HARVEY FERGUSON, *Rio Grande,* 1933

MAYNARD DIXON, Open Range, 1942, Oil on canvas, 40 x 36 inches

MAYNARD DIXON
1942 ©

LEW DAVIS, Little Boy Lives in a Copper Camp, 1939, Oil on masonite, 29½ x 24½ inches

PHILIP LATIMER DIKE, Copper, c. 1936, Oil on canvas, 38⅛ x 46¼ inches   103

JOELLYN DUESBERRY. Dixon's Orchard, La Cañada, 1986, Oil on linen, 24 x 36 inches

THEODORE VAN SOELEN. Shadows, n.d., Oil on canvas, 36⅛ x 40 inches (*opposite*)

MORRIS RIPPEL. The Spirits of the Basket Makers, 1982, Egg tempera, 18 x 30 inches

PHILIP PEARLSTEIN. Monument Valley, 1976, Watercolor on paper, 29 x 41 inches (*opposite*)

WILSON HURLEY, Thunderhead East of Domingo Baca Canyon, Oil on canvas, 50 x 76 inches

P. A. NISBET, Ship of Stone, 1992, Oil on canvas, 23 x 38 inches (*opposite*)

MOST OF NEW MEXICO, MOST OF THE YEAR,

is an indescribable harmony in browns and grays, over which the enchanted light of its blue
skies casts an eternal spell. Its very rocks are unique — only Arizona shares those astounding
freaks of form and color carved by the scant rains and more liberal winds of
immemorial centuries, and towering across the bare land like the
milestones of forgotten giants.

CHARLES LUMMIS, *The Land of Poco Tiempo*, 1893

IN the desert,
I saw a creature, naked, bestial,
Who, squatting upon the ground,
Held his heart in his hands,
And ate of it.
I said: "Is it good, friend?"
"It is bitter—bitter," he answered;
"But I like it
Because it is bitter,
And because it is my heart."

STEPHEN CRANE, *In the Desert*, 1894

JAMES DOOLIN, Last Painter on Earth, 1983, Oil on canvas, 72 x 120 inches

I WENT IN SEARCH OF ASTRAL AMERICA...

the America of the empty...the America of desert speed...to understand it,

you have to take to the road, to that travelling which achieves...the aesthetics of

disappearance....For the desert is simply that:...an ecstatic form of disappearance.

JEAN BAUDRILLARD, *America*, 1986

DAVID HOCKNEY, Arizona, 1964, Acrylic on canvas, 60 x 60 inches

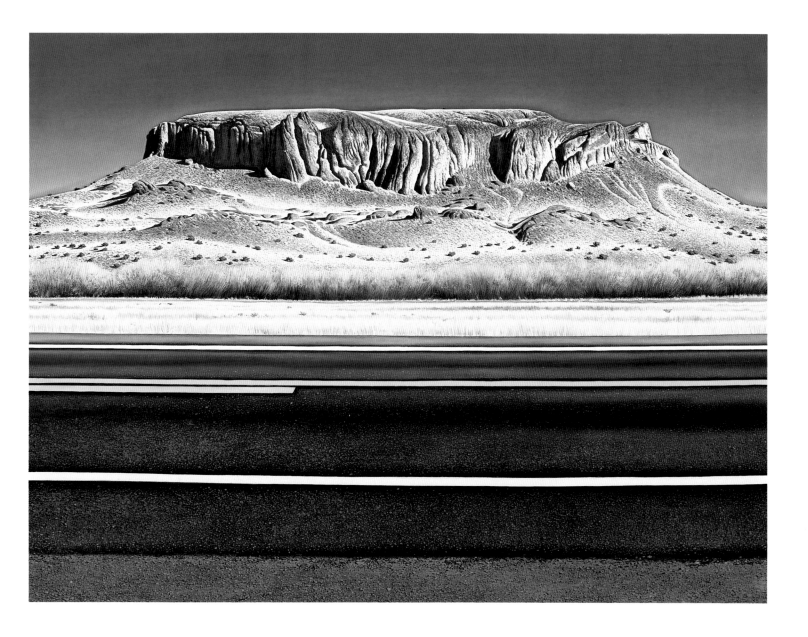

WOODY GWYN, Highway and Mesa, 1982, Oil with alkyd resins on linen, 60 x 78 inches

As NIGHT IS FALLING, AFTER THREE HOURS DRIVING,
I am lost...driving on and on towards the last of the sun's rays, then by the headlights
reflecting in the sand of the river bed....Darkness is falling all around: the prospect
of spending the night here looms, but the whisky creates a delicious sense of abandon.

JEAN BAUDRILLARD, *America,* 1986

JAMES DOOLIN, Highway at Night, 1984, Oil on canvas, 72 x 96 inches

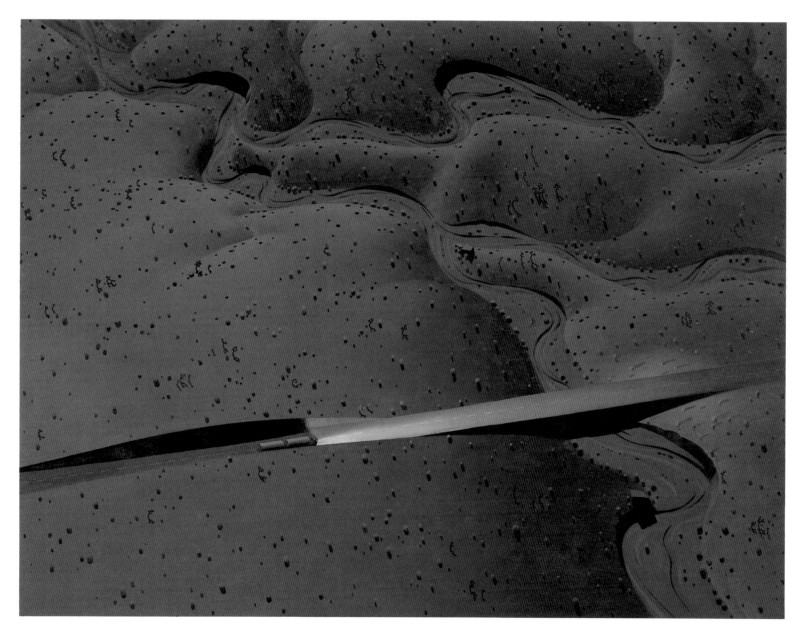

WATCHING a cloud on the desert,
Endlessly watching small insects crawl in and
    out of the shadow of a cactus.
. . .

Uninterrupted sky and blown sand:
Space — volume — silence —
Nothing but life on the desert,
Intense life.

ALICE CORBIN HENDERSON
Four O'clock in the Afternoon, 1920

MAYNARD DIXON, Saguaros at Sunset, 1925, Oil on canvas, 30 x 25 inches

JOHN FINCHER, *West of Roswell*, 1993, Oil on canvas, 64 x 94 inches

ELMER SCHOOLEY, Hot Country, 1983 – 85, Oil on canvas, 80 x 90 inches

BARBARA ZARING, Red Rock / Blue Sky, 1990, Oil on linen, 48 x 60 inches

Artists' Biographies

KENNETH MILLER ADAMS (1897–1981). Born in Topeka, Kansas; moved to New Mexico in 1924. Youngest, last and most modern member of Taos Society of Artists (TSA). Noted for landscapes and sympathetic paintings of Hispanics.

LOUIS AKIN (1868–1913). Born near Corvallis, Oregon. Went to Arizona in 1903 to paint Hopi Indians; lived among them. Hopis and Grand Canyon his favorite subjects.

MARIA BACA (b. 1951). Native of Albuquerque, New Mexico. Introduced to art in childhood as means of communication with her English-speaking teacher. Portrays life in the Barelas barrio. Has exhibited her work nationally since 1981.

JOZEF G. BAKÓS (1891–1977). Buffalo, New York native. In 1920, went to Santa Fe, cofounded Los Cinco Pintores. Deeply personal work shows modernist influences.

GEORGE BELLOWS (1882–1925). New York-based realist painter, visited Santa Fe in 1917 with fellow New York artist Robert Henri. Held exhibit at Museum of Fine Arts; never returned to Southwest.

THOMAS BENRIMO (1887–1958). Born in San Francisco. Commercial artist, set designer, moved to Taos in 1939 to devote time to painting. First in art colony to adopt surrealist style.

THOMAS HART BENTON (1889–1975). Regionalist active in New York, later in Missouri. Traveled widely; visited Southwest in 1926.

OSCAR E. BERNINGHAUS (1874–1952). Largely self-taught, toured Southwest in 1899, returned every summer until 1925, then settled permanently. One of six founders of TSA in 1915. Known as painter of Indians and southwestern landscape.

EMIL BISTTRAM (1895–1976). Left Hungary to work as artist in New York. Traveled to Taos, New Mexico, then Mexico to study fresco with Diego Rivera. In 1938 founded New Mexico Transcendental Artists group; in 1952 cofounded Taos Art Association.

ERNEST L. BLUMENSCHEIN (1874–1960). Traveled to Taos with Bert Phillips in 1898. In 1919, moved permanently to Taos. Cofounded TSA, and was frequently its spokesman.

HOMER BOSS (1882–1956). Born in Massachusetts, studied in New York with William Merritt Chase, Robert Henri. Showed at 1913 Armory Show; taught at Art Students League, Parsons School of Design. Visited New Mexico in 1925 and 1933.

PAUL BURLIN (1886–1969). New Yorker, exhibited in 1913 Armory Show. Spent much of 1913 to 1920 in Santa Fe, introduced Fauve and Expressionist distortions of form and color to New Mexico art.

GERALD CASSIDY (1879–1934). Studied at Art Students League in New York, pursued commercial art career. Settled in Santa Fe in 1912. Painted murals in 1915 Panama-California International Exposition. Paintings of Indian and desert life.

HOWARD COOK (1901–1980). Studied with Andrew Dasburg. Traveled to Taos in 1926 to illustrate Willa Cather's *Death Comes for the Archbishop*. Met and married artist Barbara Latham. Settled in Taos in 1935, portrayed landscape and Pueblo Indians in abstract style.

ANDREW DASBURG (1887–1979). Born in Paris, came to U.S. as a child. Visited Gertrude Stein in Paris; showed Cézanne-inspired work at 1913 Armory Show. In 1918, visited Mabel Dodge Luhan; settled permanently in New Mexico in 1933. Employed modified cubism in Southwest landscapes.

LEW DAVIS (1910–1979). Born in copper-mining town of Jerome, Arizona. Studied in New York, returned to Arizona in 1937. A Regionalist, he depicted the conditions in depressed mining towns.

STUART DAVIS (1894–1964). Friend of realist artists John Sloan and Robert Henri. At invitation of Sloan, spent summer of 1923 in New Mexico, painted humorous, modernist-influenced landscapes.

PHIL DIKE (1906–1990). Southern California regionalist of 1930s and 1940s; best known for city views; active in California Watercolor Society; also teacher and color advisor for animated film studios.

MAYNARD DIXON (1875–1946). California native. Cofounder, California Society of Artists, San Francisco Art Students League. In 1900, painted through Southwest; returned 1902. Married photographer Dorothea Lange in 1920. Last work was mural of Grand Canyon for the SFRR's Los Angeles ticket office.

JAMES DOOLIN (b. 1932). Born in Hartford, Connecticut; has lived in California since receiving an MFA from UCLA in 1971; known for his desert and urban landscapes.

JOELLYN DUESBERRY (b. 1944). Virginia native, studied at Smith College, Art Students League; became art appraiser. First painted New Mexico landscape in 1985; lives in northern New Mexico.

WILLIAM HERBERT "BUCK" DUNTON (1878–1936). Worked as cowboy, became commercial illustrator of western scenes. Ernest Blumenschein urged him to visit Taos, where he remained to portray wildlife and rugged mountain men.

MAX ERNST (1891–1976). Prominent in Dada and Surrealist movements, German-born artist visited Sedona, Arizona in 1943. Lived there from 1946, painting surrealist-inspired landscapes.

JOHN FINCHER (b. 1941). Born in Hamilton, Texas, received his MFA at the University of Oklahoma. Abandoning traditional, realist painting, moved to Santa Fe in 1976 to paint the "New West."

ALYCE FRANK (b. 1932). Louisiana-born, traveled extensively, worked in California as educational film editor. Moved to Taos in 1962, began painting in 1973; founder, Taos Expressionist Group.

WOODY GWYN (b. 1924). Native of San Antonio, Texas. After working as a Texas artist for many years, moved to Santa Fe in the late 1970s "for the light" and to paint landscapes.

MARSDEN HARTLEY (1877–1943). American modernist. Traveled to Europe with Alfred Stieglitz, met Wassily Kandinsky, Franz Marc, other Blaue Reiter artists. Visited Taos and Santa Fe, 1918, 1919. Painted New Mexico landscapes in Berlin, 1920s.

E. MARTIN HENNINGS (1866–1956). New Jersey native. Visited Taos, 1917; became permanent resident, 1921. Stylized, decorative paintings of Indians in landscape won many national prizes.

VELINO SHIJE HERRERA (MA-PE-WI) (1902–1973). Born Zia Pueblo, New Mexico; self-taught, began painting career, 1917. Blended tradition and innovation in scenes of Pueblo life; leader in Indian watercolor movement.

VICTOR HIGGINS (1884–1949). Studied at Art Institute of Chicago. Traveled to New Mexico, 1914. Divided time between Taos and Chicago; link between conservative and modernist artists in New Mexico.

DAVID HOCKNEY (b. 1937). First exhibited paintings, 1960; became leading exponent of Pop Art in native England, influenced by American Pop Art. Traveled through Southwest in 1964.

ALEXANDER HOGUE (b. 1898). Texas native, visited Taos, 1926–1942. Known for Dust Bowl scenes of 1930s. Interested in Pueblo spiritual concerns; work reveals abstract metaphysical investigations.

WILLIAM HENRY HOLMES (1846–1933). Ohio native. Compiled superb collection of drawings and watercolors of Grand Canyon during 1880 expedition. Combines scientific eye, aesthetic sensitivity. Director, National Gallery of Art, from 1920.

EDWARD HOPPER (1882–1967). Prominent regionalist painter affiliated with Robert Henri, other realists in New York. Visited New Mexico only once, in 1925; was not attracted by Southwest landscape.

PETER HURD (1904–1984). Born in Roswell, New Mexico, studied with N.C. Wyeth, married Wyeth's daughter, Henriette. Egg tempera medium gives his paintings an atmospheric quality typical of the Southwest's light and color.

WILSON HURLEY (b. 1924). As a child, visited studios of Santa Fe artists Theodore Van Soelen and Jozef Bakós. After painting as a pastime, decided at age 40 to become a full-time artist. Now recognized as a leading landscape painter.

REBECCA SALSBURY JAMES (1891–1968). American, born London, became member of Alfred Stieglitz circle after marriage to photographer Paul Strand. Self-taught, painted reverse oils on glass. Traveled with Georgia O'Keeffe to New Mexico, 1929; returned permanently to Taos, 1934.

RICHARD KERN (1821–1853). One of three artist/scientist brothers from Philadelphia who helped in the exploration and documentation of the Southwest. Richard was among the first artists to visit northern New Mexico, filling his sketch book with watercolors of the rugged landscape.

LEON KROLL (1884–1974). Encouraged by Winslow Homer to become artist, studied at Art Students League, then in Paris; exhibited in 1913 Armory Show. Influenced by Robert Henri circle. Made one brief visit to Santa Fe, 1917.

PAUL LANTZ (b. 1908). Born in Nebraska; painted in New Mexico from 1930 to 1939. Active in WPA-sponsored art projects; painted many murals in the Southwest. Lives in Phoenix, Arizona.

BARBARA LATHAM (1896–1989). Visited Mabel Dodge Luhan in Taos, 1924; moved there, 1925; met and married artist Howard Cook. Studies with Andrew Dasburg led to Cubist-inspired paintings of Pueblo ceremonials, local landscape.

WILLIAM R. LEIGH (1866–1955). Born in West Virginia. As illustrator for *Scribner's*, was sent to Southwest. Favorite subjects were lands of the Hopi and Navajo. Paintings of Grand Canyon earned him label "Romantic Realist."

JOHN MARIN (1870–1953). American watercolorist, visited Taos in 1929 and 1930 as guest of Mabel Dodge Luhan. Prolific watercolors of New Mexico landscape and Indian rituals influenced many artists, especially Andrew Dasburg and Victor Higgins.

FRANK MASON (b. 1921). Instructor of Fine Arts at Art Students League, teaches and paints in the grand tradition of the Old Masters. Frequent trips to Southwest, does en plein-air painting.

ILA McAFEE (b. 1897). Childhood on Colorado ranch instilled a love of horses, her principal subject. Visiting Taos in 1926, she and husband, painter Elmer Turner, made it their permanent home.

WILLARD MIDGETTE (1937–1978). Participating in the U.S. Dept. of Interior's art project, "America 1976," gave Midgette opportunity to interpret contemporary Southwest culture.

THOMAS MORAN (1837–1926). Born in Great Britain, came to U.S. at age 7. Grand Canyon became a favorite subject. Called the father of Taos art colony, for inspiring Ernest Blumenschein and Bert Phillips to travel there in 1898.

WILLARD NASH (1898–1943). Traveled to Santa Fe, 1920. Andrew Dasburg introduced him to work of Cézanne, which influenced his New Mexico landscapes. Cofounder of Los Cinco Pintores.

P. A. NISBET (b. 1949). Pennsylvanian, fell in love with the desert; in 1980 moved to Southwest. Influenced by the Luminists, paints landscapes, desert storms, clouds, and other natural phenomena.

B. J. O. NORDFELDT (1878–1955). Emigrating to Chicago in 1891 from Sweden, moved to Santa Fe in 1919; lived there for twenty years. Influenced by Cézanne and Fauves.

GEORGIA O'KEEFFE (1887–1986). Midwesterner. Promoted as truly American artist by patron, then husband Alfred Stieglitz. Trip to New Mexico in 1929 began a lifelong commitment to landscape of northern New Mexico, where she returned every summer until move there permanently in 1949.

SHELDON PARSONS (1866–1943). New York painter. Tuberculosis patient, moved to New Mexico. Recovered in Santa Fe, began painting landscapes. First director, Museum of Fine Arts, Santa Fe, 1917.

PHILIP PEARLSTEIN (b. 1924). Career began in 1950s as an Abstract Expressionist. Fascinated with ancient ruins of Southwest, he traveled to Arizona to paint architectural and natural monuments as part of "America 1976" project.

BERT GEER PHILLIPS (1868–1956). Studied at New York Art Students League and National Academy of Design. On a trip with fellow student Ernest Blumenschein to Taos, he established Taos art colony. Painted romantic scenes of Indian, Hispanic life.

MORRIS RIPPEL (b. 1930). Architect, began painting full-time in 1967. Albuquerque native, strives for total realism in his egg tempera landscapes, painted on site in New Mexico and Arizona.

FRITZ SCHOLDER (b. 1937). Born in Minnesota, of Native American heritage (on his father's side), paints in expressionist style. Moved to Taos in 1964. Combination of traditional Indian subjects and contemporary style has made him a leader of the new Indian painting movement.

ELMER SCHOOLEY (b. 1916). Born in Lawrence, Kansas; came to New Mexico in 1946. Taught arts and crafts for 30 years. A lithographer, etcher and painter, lives with wife, painter Gussie Du Jardin.

JOSEPH HENRY SHARP (1859–1953). Traveled to New Mexico in 1893 to illustrate magazine article; moved there in 1912. Charter member, Taos Society of Artists, recorded disappearing Indian culture.

JOHN SLOAN (1871–1951). Participated in 1908 Macbeth Gallery show of The Eight; Armory Show of 1913. Visited Santa Fe in 1919; returned every summer, where his palette brightened in response to light and color of New Mexico landscape.

HAUGHTON CRANFORD SMITH (1887–1983). Traveled in Europe and South America. During 1920s painted in Santa Fe and Taos. Befriended Indians, who inspired many of his Southwest paintings.

JOHN MIX STANLEY (1814–1872). Traveled through Arizona in 1846 as artist for Army of the West during Mexican War. Dream of recording American Indian tribes ended when all but five works burned in Smithsonian Institution fire in 1865.

JULES TAVERNIER (1844–1889). Studied and exhibited in Europe, came to New York in 1872. While working for *Harper's Weekly*, commissioned to make a pictorial record of all aspects of frontier life, Indians, western migration, cattle drives, etc.

WALTER UFER (1876–1936). Lithographer, decided on art career, 1893. Went to New Mexico in 1914, gave up studio for working outdoors to create landscapes and Indian portraits. First Taos artist to win prize at Carnegie International, 1920.

THEODORE VAN SOELEN (1890–1964). Moved to New Mexico in 1916 for his health, later moved to Arizona, then Texas, to observe Indian and cowboy life. Settled in Tesuque, north of Santa Fe, rendered Southwest culture through lithographic prints, paintings, and WPA murals.

PABLITA VELARDE (b. 1918). Well-known Native American woman artist. A brilliant colorist and constant innovator, her deals mostly with women's concerns and Pueblo life. Celebrated for elaborating the earth color technique and grinding natural pigments.

GUNNAR WIDFORSS (1879–1934). Swedish-born master watercolorist became "painter of the National Parks." Settled in California, 1921, traveled all over West; favorite subject was Grand Canyon.

HENRIETTE WYETH (b. 1907). Daughter of famous illustrator N.C. Wyeth. Married father's student Peter Hurd, settled with him in San Patricio, New Mexico, where she still lives. Primarily known for portraits and still lifes.

BARBARA ZARING (b. 1925). Born in Ohio, moved to Taos in 1973 to devote her life to art. Influenced by German Expressionism and the Fauves, noted for joyful, boldly colorful landscapes.

Selected Southwest Museums

THE ALBUQUERQUE MUSEUM: ART, HISTORY AND SCIENCE
2000 Mountain Road NW
Albuquerque, NM 87104
Tel. 505-243-7255

The Albuquerque Museum is located in the heart of historic Old Town and just across the street from the New Mexico Museum of Natural History. The Museum's history and art collections feature items from all over the world but focus on New Mexico and the Southwest. The Southwest encompasses a dynamic blend of Native American, Hispanic, and Anglo cultures, and The Albuquerque Museum offers a view and understanding of the four centuries of Albuquerque history and the important role each culture has played in the creation of the city. Collections include paintings by New Mexico artists from the early 20th century to the present: a significant Georgia O'Keeffe painting, *Grey Cross with Blue*; a historic photo-archive containing over 60,000 images; a 1911 Curtiss-type biplane; and a nationally recognized Spanish Colonial arms and armour collection. Museum tours may be arranged by calling ahead.

The Albuquerque Museum is accessible to persons with mobility disabilities. If you require other forms of assistance, please call (505) 243-7255 (voice) or (505) 764-6556 (TDD) at least five business days ahead.

Hours & Admission: Tues. – Sun. 9:00 – 5:00; closed Mondays, Christmas, New Year's Day, and other city holidays. Admission is free.

TUCSON MUSEUM OF ART & HISTORIC BLOCK
140 N. Main, Tucson, AZ 85701
Tel. 602-624-2333

In 1776 soldiers mustered for patrols and inspections in the central presidio of Tucson. From inside their fortress, the Spanish military protected the area from frequent Apache raids. Today the Tucson Museum of Art and five historic homes are located on a block in the heart of the old presidio. The Museum houses an outstanding permanent collection that includes pre-Columbian art and artifacts, Spanish colonial art, American western art, and 20th-century European and American art. The Museum Gift Shop in the main gallery is nationally known for its unique southwestern arts and crafts. Built within the original presidio wall, La Casa Cordova — the first of the historic homes — is one of Tucson's oldest buildings. Inside the house is a diorama of the presidio, two period rooms restored and furnished as they were in the 1800s, and a magnificent Nativity scene, which tells the story of Christmas and depicts the rich scenes of Mexican folk life. The Corbett House, dating back to the late 1800s, is currently being restored to its original state. The Fish and Stevens houses, built in the 1880s, presently house a southwestern art gallery and one of Tucson's finest restaurants. The Romero House currently houses The Museum Gift Shop Annex. The Museum has extensive educational programs including an art school, docent-led tours, lectures, and presentations to the community and schools.

Hours & Admission: Mon. – Sat. 10:00 – 5:00; Sun. 12:00 – 4:00 (Sept. – May); closed Mondays (June – Aug). Free for members and children under 12; $2 for adults; $1 for seniors and students. Free to everyone on Tuesdays.

THE HARWOOD FOUNDATION MUSEUM
238 Ledoux Street
Taos, NM 87571
Tel. 505-758-9826

The Harwood Foundation Museum features paintings, drawings, prints, sculpture, and photography by Taos artists. Founded in 1923 and operated by the University of New Mexico since 1936, the Harwood is the second oldest museum in the state. The Permanent Collection includes 19th-century *retablos* (religious paintings on wood) and works by 20th-century artists. Many of the best known artists of Taos are represented from the early days of the art colony with Victor Higgins, Ernest Blumenschein, and other members of the Taos Society of Artists. In addition, special changing exhibitions take place several times each year, providing a showcase for today's leading artists such as Larry Bell, Edward Corbett, Agnes Martin, Louis Ribak, and Earl Stroh. Located at the west end of Ledoux Street within walking distance of Taos Plaza, the historic adobe compound that houses the Harwood dates back to the mid-19th century. It has been a landmark since Burt and Elizabeth Harwood bought the property in 1916 and made it into one of the first and finest examples of "Pueblo Revival" architecture. Southwest architect John Gaw Meem oversaw its further expansion in 1937. The Harwood is listed on the National Register of Historic Places.

Hours & Admission: Mon. – Fri. 12:00 – 5:00; Sat. 10:00 – 4:00; closed major holidays. Admission is free.

THE ROSWELL MUSEUM AND ART CENTER
100 West 11th Street
Roswell, NM 88201
Tel. 505-624-6744

Celebrated for the excellence of its collections and exhibitions, The Roswell Museum and Art Center is one of the Southwest's premiere cultural attractions. A treasure house of exploration and discovery in sixteen galleries, the museum houses an impressive collection of historic and contemporary fine arts, including works by Georgia O'Keeffe, Marsden Hartley, Peter Hurd, Henriette Wyeth, and many of the Taos and Santa Fe masters. The region's multicultural history is echoed by the Rogers Aston Collection of Native American and Western Art. Also notable is the Dr. Robert H. Goddard Collection of experimental liquid-fueled rocketry, an exhibit that recounts Goddard's pioneering experiments in Roswell from 1930 to 1941. An active temporary exhibition schedule supports the collections with illuminating examples of Native American, Hispanic, and Anglo art and artifacts. Docent tours are available for adults and children with two weeks advance notice and scheduling.

Hours & Admission: Mon. – Sat. 9:00 – 5:00; Sundays and holidays 1:00 – 5:00; closed Thanksgiving, Christmas, and New Year's Day. There is no admission charge, but donations are welcome.

THE MUSEUM OF FINE ARTS
104 W. Palace Avenue
Santa Fe, NM 87501
Tel. 505-827-4468

Established in 1917, the Museum of Fine Arts is one of four museums in Santa Fe administered by the Museum of New Mexico. Artists attracted by the light and clear mountain air of the Rockies began to cluster in Santa Fe in the early 1900s, quickly outgrowing their painting and exhibition space at the next-door Palace of the Governors. The Museum of Fine Arts' permanent collection of 8,000 paintings, prints, drawings, photographs, and sculpture includes works by Georgia O'Keeffe, William Penhallow Henderson, Gene Kloss, Józef Bakós, Gustave Baumann, Robert Henri, John Sloan, Laura Gilpin, Bruce Naumann, and Allan Houser among many others. The museum stands in the vanguard of contemporary regional art, mounting at least two shows yearly of emerging artists. The museum's biennial juried exhibition attracts entries from all over the Southwest. The building itself, perhaps the most photographed structure in Santa Fe, is an outstanding example of the Pueblo-revival architecture that set the standard for Santa Fe style. Its St. Francis Auditorium is host to the annual Santa Fe Chamber Music Festival and a number of outstanding lecturers and performing artists.

Hours & Admission: 10:00 – 5:00 daily; closed Mondays in January and February, and major holidays. $5 for three-day pass to all four MNM museums; $4 for adult admission to one museum. Children under 17 free.

PHOENIX ART MUSEUM
1625 N. Central Avenue
Phoenix, AZ 85004
Tel. 602-257-1222

The Southwest's largest art museum features exhibitions of painting, sculpture, and photography as well as historic clothing and decorative objects dating from the Renaissance to today. The Museum's collection includes significant Asian, European, Western American, Latin American, and contemporary art and costume, plus the famous Thorne Miniature Rooms of historic interiors. Highlights of the collection include works by William Merritt Chase, Claude Monet, Pablo Picasso, Georgia O'Keeffe, Auguste Rodin, Thomas Moran, Frederic Remington, and Frida Kahlo. Tours of the Museum and midday gallery talks are offered daily. The art reference library, which houses more than 40,000 books, monographs, magazines, exhibition catalogs, and auction records, is open Tuesday through Friday. The Museum Store features a fascinating selection of unique gifts, jewelry, art books, cards, exhibition posters, children's toys, and more.

Hours & Admission: Tues. – Sat. 10:00 – 5:00; Wed. 10:00 – 9:00; Sun. 12:00 – 5:00; closed Mondays and major holidays. Free for members, children under 6, and school tours; $4 for adults; $3 for adults 65 and older; $1.50 for children 6 and older, and full-time students. Free to everyone on Wednesdays.

Credits

Adams, Kenneth Miller
The Dry Ditch, 1964
Oil on canvas, 50 x 36 inches
Eiteljorg Museum of American Indian and Western Art
Indianapolis, IN
28

Akin, Louis
Mesa and Desert, 1905
Oil on canvas, 30 x 36 inches
Collection of Mr. & Mrs. Bertrand G. Babbitt
7

Baca, Maria
Paisaje en Verano, 1991
Oil on canvas, 66 x 72 inches
Private collection
27

Bakós, Józef G.
El Sanctuário, Chimayó, before 1940
Oil on canvas, 30 x 34 inches
The Anschutz Collection
Photograph: James O. Milmoe
38

Bellows, George Wesley
Pueblo, Tesuque, Number One, 1917
Oil on canvas, 34 x 44 inches
The Anschutz Collection
Photograph: James O. Milmoe
39

Benrimo, Thomas
White Moon Number Two, c. 1954
Oil on masonite, 32 x 48 inches
The Harwood Foundation Museum, Taos, NM
93

Benton, Thomas Hart
New Mexico, 1926
Oil and egg tempera on board, 20¼ x 26¼ inches
Denver Art Museum
68

Berninghaus, Oscar E.
A Showery Day, Grand Canyon, 1915
Oil on canvas, 30 x 40 inches
The Santa Fe Collection of Southwestern Art, Chicago
32

Berninghaus, Oscar E.
Haytime and Showers, 1940
Oil on canvas, 35 x 40 inches
Private collection, Taos, NM
Photograph: Gordon Adams
71

Bisttram, Emil
Church at Ranchos, c. 1930
Watercolor on paper, 13½ x 19½ inches
Photograph courtesy of the Gerald Peters Gallery
Santa Fe, NM
80

Bisttram, Emil
Nature Rhythms, 1958
Watercolor on paper, 18¼ x 22 inches
Courtesy of Zaplin-Lampert Gallery, Santa Fe, NM
96

Blumenschein, Ernest L.
Afternoon of a Sheep Herder, n.d.
Oil on canvas, 28 x 50 inches
National Cowboy Hall of Fame and
Western Heritage Center
91

Blumenschein, Ernest L.
Sangre de Cristo Mountains, 1925
Oil on canvas, 50¼ x 60 inches
The Anschutz Collection
Photograph: James O. Milmoe
20

Blumenschein, Ernest L.
The Lake, n.d.
Oil on canvas, 24⅛ x 27 inches
National Academy of Design, NY
57

Boss, Homer
Red Clay Formation, c. 1920s
Oil on canvas, 26 x 32 inches
Photograph courtesy of the Gerald Peters Gallery
Santa Fe, NM
48

Burlin, Paul
Grand Canyon, n.d.
Oil on canvas, 20 x 25 inches
The Harmsen Collection
58

Cassidy, Gerald
Cui Bono?, c. 1911
Oil on canvas, 93½ x 48 inches
Museum of Fine Arts, Museum of New Mexico
Santa Fe, NM, Gift of Gerald Cassidy
21

Cook, Howard
Winter Mountain, Cycle No. 4, 1955
Oil on canvas, 26 x 55 inches
Museum of Fine Arts, Museum of New Mexico
Santa Fe, NM, Gift of Howard Cook in Memory
of Dr. Reginald Fisher, 1978
64

Dasburg, Andrew
New Mexican Village, 1926
Oil on canvas, 24 x 30 inches
Museum of Fine Arts, Museum of New Mexico
Santa Fe, NM, Gift of Cyrus McCormick
73

Dasburg, Andrew
New Mexico Landscape, 1932
Watercolor, 19 x 22 inches
Photograph courtesy of the Gerald Peters Gallery
Santa Fe, NM
94

Davis, Lew
Little Boy Lives in a Copper Camp, 1939
Oil on masonite, 29½ x 24½ inches
Phoenix Art Museum
Gift of I.B.M. Corporation
102

Davis, Stuart
New Mexico Gate, 1923
Oil on linen, 22 x 32 inches
Permanent Collection, Roswell Museum and
Art Center, Roswell, NM
Gift of Mr. & Mrs. Donald Winston and
Mr. & Mrs. Samuel H. Marshall
Half-title page

WALTER UFER. *Oferta para San Esquipula*, 1918, Oil on canvas, 25 x 30 inches

Dike, Philip Latimer
Copper, c. 1936
Oil on canvas, 38⅛ x 46¼ inches
Phoenix Art Museum
Western Art Associates Purchase
103

Dixon, Maynard
Cloud World, 1925
Oil on canvas, 34 x 62 inches
Courtesy of Arizona West Galleries, Scottsdale
Title page

Dixon, Maynard
Desert Southwest, 1944
Oil on canvas, 40 x 36 inches
The Anschutz Collection
Photograph: James O. Milmoe
75

Dixon, Maynard
Saguaros At Sunset, 1925
Oil on canvas, 30 x 25 inches
Private collection
Photograph courtesy of Mitchell, Brown
Gallery, Inc., Santa Fe, NM
117

Dixon, Maynard
Open Range, 1942
Oil on canvas, 40 x 36 inches
Museum of Western Art, Denver, CO
101

Doolin, James
Highway at Night, 1984
Oil on canvas, 72 x 96 inches
Courtesy of Koplin Gallery, Santa Monica, CA
115

Doolin, James
Last Painter on Earth, 1983
Oil on canvas, 72 x 120 inches
Courtesy of Koplin Gallery, Santa Monica, CA
110

Duesberry, Joellyn
Dixon's Orchard, La Cañada, 1986
Oil on linen, 24 x 36 inches
Photograph courtesy of the Gerald Peters Gallery
Santa Fe, NM
105

Dunton, William Herbert "Buck"
Sunset in the Foothills, n.d.
Oil on canvas, 40 x 50 inches
Nelda C. Stark, Orange, TX
46

Dunton, William Herbert "Buck"
The Cattlebuyer, 1922
Oil on canvas, 50 x 60 inches
Nelda C. Stark, Orange, TX
47

Ernst, Max
Colline inspirée (Inspired Hill), 1950
Oil and canvas, 28¾ x 36¼ inches
The Menil Collection, Houston, TX
Photograph: Paul Hester
92

Fincher, John
West of Roswell, 1993
Oil on canvas, 64 x 94 inches
Courtesy of Elaine Horwitch Galleries
117

Frank, Alyce
Morada by Mabel Dodge House, 1989
Oil on linen, 30 x 40 inches
Private collection
6

Gwyn, Woody
Highway and Mesa, 1982
Oil with alkyd resins on linen, 60 x 78 inches
Museum of Fine Arts, Museum of New Mexico
Santa Fe, NM, Museum Purchase
113

Hartley, Marsden
Cemetery New Mexico, 1922-24
Oil on canvas, 31⅛ x 39¼ inches
The Metropolitan Museum of Art, NY
The Alfred Stieglitz Collection
12

Hartley, Marsden
Desert Scene, c. 1922
Oil on board, 25¾ x 31⅞ inches
Eiteljorg Museum of American Indian and Western Art
Indianapolis, IN
51

Hartley, Marsden
Landscape: New Mexico, 1920
Oil on composition board, 25⅜ x 29¼ inches
Permanent Collection, Roswell Museum and Art Center
Roswell, NM, Gift of Ione & Hudson Walker
62

Hartley, Marsden
Landscape No. 3, (Cash Entry Mines,
New Mexico), 1920
Oil on canvas, 27¾ x 35¾ inches

Photograph © 1993, The Art Institute of Chicago
All Rights Reserved
Alfred Stieglitz Collection, 1949.549
63

Hennings, E. Martin
Through the Chamisa, c. 1920s
Oil on canvas, 45 x 43 inches
Courtesy of Nedra Matteucci's Fenn Galleries
Santa Fe, NM
70

Herrera, Velino Shije, (Ma-Pe-Wi)
Buffalo Hunt, c. 1930
Watercolor on paper, 25 x 29½ inches
School of American Research, Santa Fe, NM
22

Higgins, Victor
Mountain Forms #2, c. 1924-27
Oil on canvas, 40½ x 43 inches
National Museum of American Art
Smithsonian Institution, Gift of Arvin Gottlieb
Photograph courtesy of Art Resource, NY
(The Smithsonian Institution makes no representation
as to copyright status for this work)
79

Higgins, Victor
Spring Rain, c. 1924
Oil on canvas, 40 x 43 inches
© 1992 The Art Institute of Chicago
All Rights Reserved
Friends of American Art Collection, 1924.18
61

Higgins, Victor
Taos Valley, c. 1932-35
Oil on canvas, 54 x 60 inches
The Snite Museum of Art
University of Notre Dame, Notre Dame, IN
Gift of Mr. John T. Higgins, 63.53.3
98

Hockney, David
Arizona, 1964
Acrylic on canvas, 60 x 60 inches
© David Hockney
112

Hogue, Alexandre
Procession of the Saint—Santo Domingo, 1928
Oil on canvas, 31 x 40 inches
Nebraska Art Association, Nelle Cochrane
Woods Collection, Sheldon Memorial Art Gallery
University of Nebraska—Lincoln
1972.N-290
88

125

Holmes, William Henry
Cliff House in 1875, 1875
Watercolor on paper, 9⅞ x 13½ inches
Peabody Museum of Archaeology & Ethnology
Harvard University, Cambridge, MA
Photograph: Hillel Burger
31

Hopper, Edward
St. Francis' Towers, Santa Fe, 1925
Watercolor on paper, 13½ x 19½ inches
© The Phillips Collection, Washington, DC
66

Hurd, Peter
Alamogordo Ranch, 1948
Egg tempera, 26 x 40 inches
The Collection of Herb & Betty Kane
Cherry Hill, NJ
Photograph courtesy of Woodrow Wilson Fine
Art, Santa Fe, NM
67

Hurley, Wilson
Thunderhead East of Domingo Baca Canyon
Oil on canvas, 50 x 76 inches
Courtesy of Nedra Matteucci's Fenn Galleries
Santa Fe, NM
108

James, Rebecca Salsbury
Earth and Water, 1950
Oil on glass, 19¾ x 16 inches
Museum of Fine Arts, Museum of New Mexico
Santa Fe, NM, Bequest of Helen Miller Jones
10

Kern, Richard H.
Valley of Taos, Looking South, N.M., 1849, 1849
Watercolor and graphite on paper, 3⅞ x 5¾ inches
Amon Carter Museum, Fort Worth
17

Kroll, Leon
Santa Fe Hills, 1917
Oil on canvas, 34 x 40¼ inches
Museum of Fine Arts, Museum of New Mexico
Santa Fe, NM, Museum Purchase
40

Lantz, Paul
Snow in Santa Fe, c. 1935
Oil on masonite, 30 x 40 inches
Museum of Fine Arts, Museum of New Mexico
Santa Fe, NM
Gift of Public Employees Retirement Act, 1972
65

Latham, Barbara
Tourist Town, Taos, 1940-49
Egg tempera on masonite, 24 x 35¾ inches
Permanent Collection, Roswell Museum and Art Center
Roswell, NM, Gift of the Artist
25

Leigh, William Robinson
Grand Canyon, 1911
Oil on canvas, 28 x 34 inches
Santa Fe Railway Collection of Southwestern Art
33

Leigh, William Robinson
Grand Canyon, 1911
Oil on canvas, 66 x 99 inches
Collection of The Newark Museum
Gift of Henry Wallington Wack, 1979
34

Marin, John
Dance of the Santo Domingo Indians, 1929
Watercolor and charcoal on paper, 22 x 30¾ inches
The Metropolitan Museum of Art, NY
The Alfred Stieglitz Collection, 1949
87

Marin, John
Near Taos, New Mexico, 1930
Watercolor on paper, 16¾ x 21½ inches
Permanent Collection, Roswell Museum
and Art Center, Roswell, NM
Gift of Mr. & Mrs. Samuel H Marshall and
Mr. & Mrs. Donald Winston
19

Marin, John
Storm over Taos, 1930
Watercolor over graphite, 15 x 20⅞ inches
© 1993 National Gallery of Art, Washington
Alfred Stieglitz Collection
60

Mason, Frank
Fisherman, Santa Fe, 1983
Oil on canvas, 18 x 24 inches
Private collection
128

Mcafee, Ila
Antelope, n.d.
Oil on canvas, 39½ x 45½ inches
Albuquerque High School Collection
Gift of the Class of 1934
18

Midgette, Willard
Processing Sheep, 1976
Oil on linen, 108¼ x 156½ inches
Phoenix Art Museum
Museum Purchase with funds provided by
Mr. & Mrs. Kemper Marley
29

Moran, Thomas
Chasm of the Colorado, 1873-74
Oil on canvas, 84¾ x 144¾ inches
National Museum of American Art
Smithsonian Institution
Photograph courtesy of Art Resource, NY
14

Nash, Willard
Landscape, c. 1920s
Oil on canvas, 23¼ x 29½ inches
Courtesy of Zaplin-Lampert Gallery
Santa Fe, NM
41

Nash, Willard
Sun Mountain Abstract, 1924
Oil on canvas, 20 x 18 inches
Permanent Collection, Roswell Museum
and Art Center, Roswell, NM
Patricia Gaylord Anderson Memorial
Fund Purchase
76

Nisbet, P. A.
Ship of Stone, 1992
Oil on canvas, 23 x 38 inches
Courtesy of Frank Croft Fine Art, Santa Fe, NM
109

Nordfeldt, B. J. O.
Geophysical Forms, 1954
Oil on linen, 34 x 48 inches
Permanent Collection, Roswell Museum
and Art Center, Roswell, NM
Gift of Mrs. B. J. O. Nordfeldt
97

O'Keeffe, Georgia
Black Cross, New Mexico, 1929
Oil on canvas, 39 x 30⅜ inches
© 1993, The Art Institute of Chicago
All Rights Reserved
Art Institute Purchase Fund, 1943.95
13

I FELT RELUCTANT TO LEAVE

those brutal and rugged mountains, the dry, scorching plains, to abandon for good that
long dim trail that lay over the sandy desert like some big lazy snake asleep in the sun....
The life is wonderful, strange—the fascination of it clutches me like some unseen animal—
it seems to whisper, "Come back, you belong here, this is your real home."

N. C. WYETH, 1904

FRANK MASON, Fisherman, Santa Fe, 1983, Oil on canvas, 18 x 24 inches